This Travel Journal Belongs To

Packing Lists

Carry On

- ☐
- ☐
- ☐
- ☐
- ☐
- ☐
- ☐

Essentials

- ☐
- ☐
- ☐
- ☐
- ☐
- ☐
- ☐

Toiletries

- ☐
- ☐
- ☐
- ☐
- ☐
- ☐
- ☐

Electronics

- ☐
- ☐
- ☐
- ☐
- ☐
- ☐
- ☐

Packing Lists

Day time clothes

- ☐
- ☐
- ☐
- ☐
- ☐
- ☐
- ☐

Evening clothes

- ☐
- ☐
- ☐
- ☐
- ☐
- ☐
- ☐

Underwear etc

- ☐
- ☐
- ☐
- ☐
- ☐
- ☐
- ☐

Extras

- ☐
- ☐
- ☐
- ☐
- ☐
- ☐
- ☐

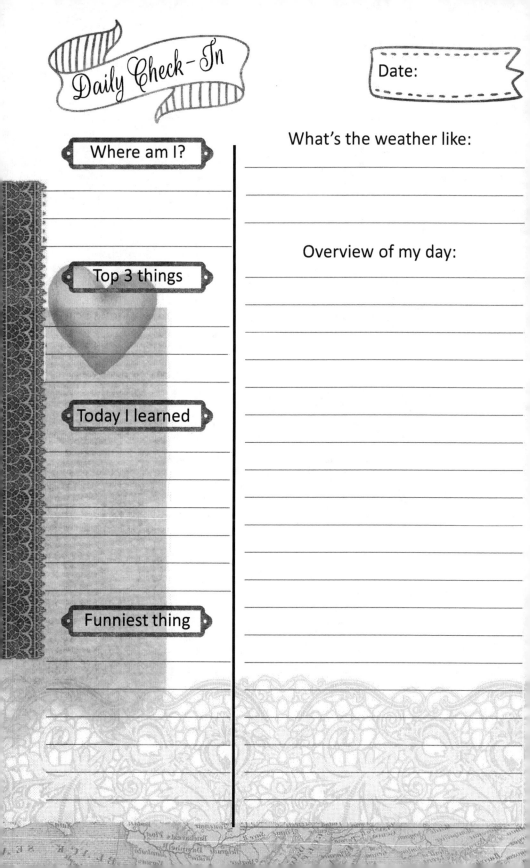

Daily Check-In

Date:

Where am I?

Top 3 things

Today I learned

Funniest thing

What's the weather like:

Overview of my day:

Tomorrow I want to...

On today's menu

Breakfast:

Lunch:

Dinner:

Interesting things

Most beautiful sight	
Favorite taste	
People I met	
Best discovery	
Best part of the day	

Happy feelings

Words that describe today

My Thoughts

My Thoughts

What were your first impressions when you arrived?

Have you forgotten anything? How have you improvised?

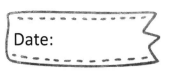

Date:

Daily Check-In

Date:

Where am I?

What's the weather like:

Top 3 things

Overview of my day:

Today I learned

Funniest thing

Tomorrow I want to...

On today's menu

Breakfast: _____

Lunch: _____

Dinner: _____

Interesting things

_____
_____
_____

Most beautiful sight	
Favorite taste	
People I met	
Best discovery	
Best part of the day	

Happy feelings

_____
_____
_____
_____
_____

Words that describe today

My Thoughts

My Thoughts

Describe the place you're staying in detail

Have there been any surprises? Write about them here

Date:

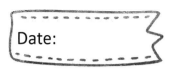

Daily Check-In

Date:

Where am I?

Top 3 things

Today I learned

Funniest thing

What's the weather like:

Overview of my day:

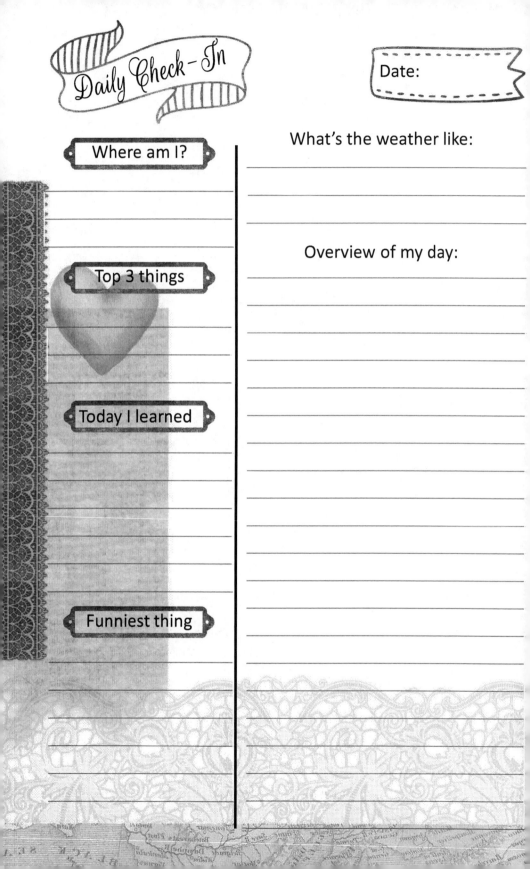

Tomorrow I want to...

On today's menu

Breakfast:

Lunch:

Dinner:

Interesting things

Most beautiful sight	
Favorite taste	
People I met	
Best discovery	
Best part of the day	

Happy feelings

Words that describe today

My Thoughts

My Thoughts

Write about all the things that are making you smile on this trip

Date:

Describe the things you can see right now

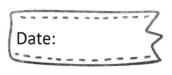

Daily Check-In

Date:

Where am I?

What's the weather like:

Top 3 things

Overview of my day:

Today I learned

Funniest thing

Tomorrow I want to...

On today's menu

Breakfast:

Lunch:

Dinner:

Interesting things

Most beautiful sight	
Favorite taste	
People I met	
Best discovery	
Best part of the day	

Happy feelings

Words that describe today

My Thoughts

My Thoughts

What is the food like? Is there anything you love/don't like?

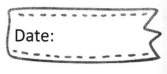

Describe any cultural differences between here and home

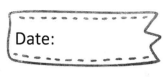

Daily Check-In

Date:

Where am I?

Top 3 things

Today I learned

Funniest thing

What's the weather like:

Overview of my day:

Tomorrow I want to...

On today's menu

Breakfast:

Lunch:

Dinner:

Interesting things

Most beautiful sight	
Favorite taste	
People I met	
Best discovery	
Best part of the day	

Happy feelings

Words that describe today

My Thoughts

My Thoughts

Write about any landmarks or special places you've visited

Write about any interesting facts you've learned

Daily Check-In

Date:

Where am I?

Top 3 things

Today I learned

Funniest thing

What's the weather like:

Overview of my day:

Tomorrow I want to...

On today's menu

Breakfast: _____

Lunch: _____

Dinner: _____

Interesting things

_____

_____

_____

Most beautiful sight	
Favorite taste	
People I met	
Best discovery	
Best part of the day	

Happy feelings

_____

_____

_____

_____

_____

Words that describe today

My Thoughts

My Thoughts

Have you met any new people? Write about them

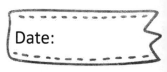

It is how you imagined it to be? Why/Why not?

Date:

_____
_____
_____
_____
_____
_____
_____
_____
_____
_____
_____
_____
_____
_____
_____
_____
_____
_____
_____
_____
_____

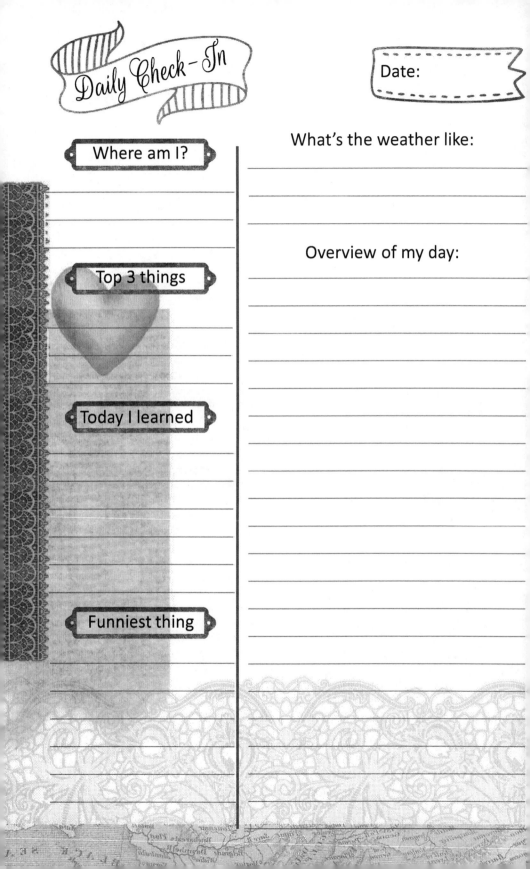

Daily Check-In

Date:

Where am I?

Top 3 things

Today I learned

Funniest thing

What's the weather like:

Overview of my day:

Tomorrow I want to...

On today's menu

Breakfast:

Lunch:

Dinner:

Interesting things

Most beautiful sight	
Favorite taste	
People I met	
Best discovery	
Best part of the day	

Happy feelings

Words that describe today

My Thoughts

My Thoughts

What were your first impressions when you arrived?

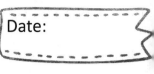

Have you forgotten anything? How have you improvised?

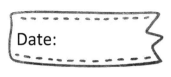

Date:

Daily Check-In

Date:

Where am I?

Top 3 things

Today I learned

Funniest thing

What's the weather like:

Overview of my day:

Tomorrow I want to...

On today's menu

Breakfast:

Lunch:

Dinner:

Interesting things

Most beautiful sight	
Favorite taste	
People I met	
Best discovery	
Best part of the day	

Happy feelings

Words that describe today

My Thoughts

My Thoughts

Describe the **place** you're staying in detail

Date:

Have there been any surprises? Write about them here

Daily Check-In

Date:

Where am I?

Top 3 things

Today I learned

Funniest thing

What's the weather like:

Overview of my day:

On today's menu

Breakfast:

Lunch:

Dinner:

Interesting things

Most beautiful sight	
Favorite taste	
People I met	
Best discovery	
Best part of the day	

Happy feelings

Words that describe today

My Thoughts

My Thoughts

Write about all the things that are making you smile on this trip

Describe the things you can see right now

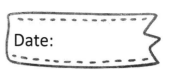

Daily Check-In

Date:

Where am I?

Top 3 things

Today I learned

Funniest thing

What's the weather like:

Overview of my day:

Tomorrow I want to...

On today's menu

Breakfast:

Lunch:

Dinner:

Interesting things

Most beautiful sight	
Favorite taste	
People I met	
Best discovery	
Best part of the day	

Happy feelings

Words that describe today

My Thoughts

My Thoughts

What is the *food* like? Is there anything you love/don't like?

Describe any cultural differences **between** here and home

Daily Check-In

Date:

Where am I?

What's the weather like:

Top 3 things

Overview of my day:

Today I learned

Funniest thing

Tomorrow I want to...

On today's menu

Breakfast:

Lunch:

Dinner:

Interesting things

Most beautiful sight	
Favorite taste	
People I met	
Best discovery	
Best part of the day	

Happy feelings

Words that describe today

My Thoughts

My Thoughts

Write about any landmarks or special *places* you've visited

Date:

Write about any interesting facts you've learned

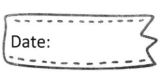

Daily Check-In

Date:

Where am I?

Top 3 things

Today I learned

Funniest thing

What's the weather like:

Overview of my day:

Tomorrow I want to...

On today's menu

Breakfast:

Lunch:

Dinner:

Interesting things

Most beautiful sight	
Favorite taste	
People I met	
Best discovery	
Best part of the day	

Happy feelings

Words that describe today

My Thoughts

My Thoughts

Have you met any new people? Write about them

Date:

_____

_____

_____

_____

_____

_____

_____

_____

_____

_____

_____

_____

_____

_____

_____

_____

_____

_____

_____

_____

_____

_____

It is how you imagined it to be? Why/Why not?

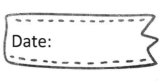

MEMORY PAGES

MAKE PICTURE COLLAGES OR DOODLE.
USE YOUR IMAGINATION!

Made in the USA
Las Vegas, NV
26 March 2024

87797889R10061